War in the Gulf

GENERAL H. NORMAN SCHWARZKOPF

Written By: Bob Italia

Published by Abdo & Daughters, 4940 Viking Drive, Edina, Minnesota 55435.

Library bound edition distributed by Rockbottom Books,
P.O. Box 398166, Minneapolis, Minnesota 55439.

Printed in the United States.
Cover photo: FPG International
Inside photos: Inside photos: Archive Photos 48
                     Bettman Archive 4, 7, 13, 23, 25, 30, 32, 35, 36, 38, 40, 44

Edited by: Rosemary Wallner

Italia, Robert, 1955-
    General H. Norman Schwarzkopf / written by Bob Italia; [edited by Rosemary
Wallner].
        p. cm. -- (War in the Gulf)
        Summary: Describes the life, accomplishments, and goals of the general who
commanded the American troops during the Persian Gulf War.
    ISBN: 1-56239-148-8 (lib ed)
    1. Schwarzkopf, H. Norman, 1934-   —Juvenile literature. 2. Generals—United
States—Biography—Juvenile literature. 3. United States. Army—Biography—Juvenile
literature. 4. Persian Gulf War, 1991—Juvenile literature. [1. Schwarzkopf, H.
Norman, 1934-   . 2. Generals.] I. Wallner, Rosemary, 1964-   . II. Title. III.
Series.
E840.5.S39182   1992   355'.0092--dc20   92-17393
                                          [B]

International Standard Book Number:	**Library of Congress Catalog Card Number:**
1-56239-148-8	92-17393

TABLE OF CONTENTS

*His success in Operation Desert Storm
made Norman Schwarzkopf a national hero.*

Stormin' Norman

H. Norman Schwarzkopf became a military hero in 1991. That year he directed the swift victory over the Iraqis in the Persian Gulf War. In January, American troops launched an air attack against Iraq. By the end of February, Iraq had surrendered. Operation Desert Storm was the code word for the invasion. Desert Storm's success restored America's pride.

Television made "Stormin' Norman" America's hero. His press briefings during the war won the hearts of American viewers. Schwarzkopf retired from the Army in August 1991. But we will hear much more from this burly and likable hero of Operation Desert Storm.

A Father's Influence

H. Norman Schwarzkopf (pronounced SHWARZ-koff) was born in Trenton, New Jersey, on August 22, 1934. His father, Herbert Norman Schwarzkopf, was the son of German immigrants. He hated the name "Herbert" so much, he gave his son the initial "H" only.

Herbert was a West Point (New York) Military Academy graduate. At the time of Schwarzkopf's birth, he headed the New Jersey State Police. When World War II started, Herbert joined the Army. He eventually became a general. He had a great influence on young Norman.

"A lot of my love of country stemmed from my father," Schwarzkopf said. "My dad was a genuine public servant. He had a deep and abiding love for his country. He wanted to serve."

Schwarzkopf's father, Herbert,
had a great influence on young Norman.

Schwarzkopf and his older sisters, Sally and Ruth Anne, grew up in Lawrenceville, a small suburb of Trenton. In 1946, twelve-year-old Schwarzkopf and his family moved to Teheran, the capital of Iran. The U.S. government had assigned Herbert to help Iran establish a national police organization.

Schwarzkopf lived in Teheran for a year. Then he attended boarding schools in Switzerland, Germany, and Italy. When he was fifteen years old, Schwarzkopf returned to America. He attended Valley Forge Military Academy in Wayne, Pennsylvania.

Mixing Football and Choir with Butter

Schwarzkopf was a bright student. He was the school's debating champion. He was also popular with the girls.

The six-foot Schwarzkopf excelled in sports. He was the football team's star tackle. And he threw the shot put for the track team. But Schwarzkopf wasn't a perfect student. Once, he was disciplined for throwing butter in the mess hall.

In 1952, Schwarzkopf graduated at the top of his class. He enrolled at West Point. Schwarzkopf wrestled and played tennis and football. He also conducted the chapel choir. In 1956, Schwarzkopf graduated in the top 10 percent of his class as a captain—the highest cadet rank possible.

After graduation, Schwarzkopf became a second lieutenant. He entered active duty. But he almost resigned.

"I had an alcoholic commander," Schwarzkopf said. "I had an executive officer who was a coward. I saw terrible things going on around me and I said, 'Who needs it? When my three years are up, I'm getting out!' But a very wise man sat me down. He said, 'If you really think it's that bad, why don't you stick around until someday you get into a position to do something about it?' "

The Specter of Vietnam

In February 1965, President Lyndon Johnson ordered U.S. troops to bomb North Vietnam. Johnson thought the U.S. should help South Vietnam defeat their enemies to the North. That year, Captain/Major Schwarzkopf was assigned to the South Vietnamese Airborne battalion. He was a task force adviser. He saw heavy action right away.

"We fought for almost every day of every month for thirteen months," he recalled. "I really thought we had done something good, just like George Washington. I had gone and fought for freedom."

When he completed his Vietnam assignment, 32-year-old Schwarzkopf flew to New York City. Still in uniform, he expected a hero's welcome. But there were no parades, no cheering crowds.

Many Americans had doubts about the Vietnam War. Some people thought Johnson should not have sent soldiers to fight. Like many Vietnam veterans, Schwarzkopf became bitter. He was angry because he had risked his life and his country did not thank him. But he didn't quit the military.

In 1967, Schwarzkopf returned to West Point to teach. He wanted to forget Vietnam for a while. While at an Army football game at West Point, he met Brenda Holsinger. She was a Trans World Airlines (TWA) flight attendant. It was love at first sight.

"Once we began dating," recalled Brenda, "I didn't go out with anyone else. Norm just seemed to have his head on straight." Schwarzkopf and Brenda married eight months later at West Point.

In 1969, Schwarzkopf received orders to return to Vietnam. He became a battalion commander with the American Division.

A year later, Schwarzkopf, twice injured in battle, found himself on the edge of death. One of his men had been severely injured in a minefield. Schwarzkopf tried to save him.

*Schwarzkopf's wife, Brenda. They met at
a West Point football game in 1967.*

Schwarzkopf ignored the danger. He inched his way to the injured soldier. He comforted the soldier until a helicopter arrived to rescue them. For his bravery, Schwarzkopf received his third Silver Star. (He also received two Purple Hearts for being wounded in action.)

Schwarzkopf stayed in Vietnam until 1970. When he returned home, America's attitude toward Vietnam veterans had turned ugly. Soldiers had bombed some Vietnam villages with napalm. Villagers—including children—had died. Many Americans were outraged.

"Ordinarily," Schwarzkopf said, "commanding an infantry battalion is the highlight of a military career. Mine wasn't...because of all the stuff going on back in the States. No one wants to go to war. But if you go, you like to know the country is behind you.

"Not only was I *not* greeted with flowers," he added, "this time I was spit upon. People were calling me a baby burner. What made it so difficult was the fact that I hadn't done any of that! There were times when I was tempted to just bail out and go build myself a cabin in the wilderness and commune with nature."

Even worse, U.S. artillery fire had killed Sergeant Michael Mullen, one of his troops. The story was made into a 1979 TV-movie "Friendly Fire." Mullen's mother personally blamed Schwarzkopf for her son's death.

"Michael's death was a terrible, terrible tragedy," Schwarzkopf said. "A tragedy typical of a profane thing called war. It's a unique thing that happens on a very occasional basis. But it happens!"

The Army studied Mullen's death. It decided Schwarzkopf was not to blame. But the tragedy still haunts him. "(Mrs. Mullen) cannot imagine how he suffered through that," said an Army colonel. "I'm certain Norman learned something from that incident. But that doesn't make it any easier for that mother."

Like most Vietnam veterans, Schwarzkopf buried the memories of war. But he didn't forget. Unlike most veterans, Schwarzkopf learned to cope with the bitterness and stayed in the military. He hoped he would one day get the chance to redeem himself in the eyes of Americans.

Another Vietnam?

In October 1983, Schwarzkopf, now a major general, received a call from his commanding officer. The army had selected Schwarzkopf for a special mission.

Twenty-four hours later, he was on the aircraft carrier *Guam,* floating around somewhere in the Caribbean Sea. He still didn't know where he was going.

"I was standing on the flight deck and the ship was kind of tossing a little bit," Schwarzkopf recalled. "The wind was blowing in my face and I thought, *Grenada!* The United States of America is about to launch a military operation into Grenada—and I'm involved!"

Four days earlier, there had been a bloody coup in the tiny West Indies island country of Grenada. The military had killed the prime minister, Maurice Bishop. The U.S. government feared that Grenada would become a Cuban communist state. The government sent troops to the island to prevent a Cuban base from being built.

"A lot of Vietnam memories came rushing back," Schwarzkopf said. "I thought, 'What am I getting myself into?' Then I thought, 'This is sort of the bottom line, the difference between being an Army officer and being in some other line of work.' I took an oath that said I would obey the *lawful* orders of my commanding officers, one of whom is the President of the United States.

"I certainly didn't know how the American people were going to take [the invasion]," he added. "But my orders were very clear to me. And I honestly don't think you have the right as an Army officer to consider that you have an opinion."

Schwarzkopf felt the Grenada operation was lawful and right. Had he felt differently, he said, "I would refuse the order [knowing] that I would be turning in my 'suit' the next day."

The Grenada operation was, for the most part, a success. In less than three days troops defeated Grenadan forces. And it was a personal success for Schwarzkopf. His work impressed the military.

"The object was to go in with what really started as an unconventional operation," Schwarzkopf said. "At the end of Day One, the whole exercise was going to be done. But [it] went sour right away. And it went sour because...we had 800 [well-armed] Cubans on the island."

The American military was criticized for taking days to defeat the Cubans. But Schwarzkopf defended his actions. He was concerned about innocent civilian lives. He ruled out the use of armored firepower.

"If it had been a conventional battle...I could have rolled into Grenada with my mechanized armor division...and blown St. George's off the map," he said. "I could have had the whole thing tied up in a neat little bundle in an hour, maybe an hour and a half. But that wasn't the nature of the operation. And it obviously would have been a terrible thing to do."

The U.S troops secured Grenada. But Schwarzkopf worried about returning to the United States. He didn't know if he could handle any criticism.

When he landed at Fort Stewart, Schwarzkopf was surprised. A small group had gathered at the airfield to welcome him. The Army band was there. So were his wife and children, Cynthia, Jessica, and Christian. Schwarzkopf was thrilled.

"I had expected to come home just the same way I came home from war the last two times," he recalled. "No big deal. But the airplane landed, the band was out there, and there were big signs saying WELCOME HOME.

"I walked out of the airplane and everybody started cheering," he added. "My wife and kids ran up and hugged me. And I didn't understand what was going on! Isn't that crazy? When it finally dawned on me, it was probably one of the greatest thrills I have ever experienced in my life."

Operation Desert Norm

Throughout 1990 Iraq's president, Saddam Hussein, gathered troops near the border of his country and Kuwait. (Kuwait is a small, oil-rich country on the Persian Gulf.) Hussein wanted to invade Kuwait and seize its oil.

By 1989 Schwarzkopf was a four-star general. That year he sensed that the U.S. would soon become involved in a Middle East conflict. He laid down the plans that would be turned into Operation Desert Shield.

Five days before Hussein invaded Kuwait, Schwarzkopf and his Central Command ran a drill. They practiced what would happen if the invasion took place. On August 2, 1990, Iraq invaded Kuwait.

Four days later, President George Bush gave the order to Schwarzkopf to send the first troops and airplanes to Saudi Arabia. Saudi Arabia is a neighbor of both Iraq and Kuwait. Bush wanted to station troops in that country to help Kuwait defeat Iraq. Operation Desert Shield had begun.

With the Saudi Arabian Ambassador to the U.S. at his side,
Schwarzkopf announces that he will direct troops in the Persian Gulf.

General Schwarzkopf was named commander in chief of the U.S. forces. From the start, he decided not to take the Iraqi Army lightly.

"Iraq had an extremely large military force," he recalled. "And we gave them credit for being ten feet tall. You know how I feel about military operations: never underestimate your enemy.

"It goes right back to the mistake we made in Grenada," he added. "I never underestimated the enemy after that experience. I look at his capabilities and assume he has them until we find out differently."

Schwarzkopf also made sure his troops did not suffer the same low morale that he did in the Vietnam War. He made trips to the front lines. He visited with troops whenever he could. Because of Schwarzkopf's visibility, the troops were eager and willing to fight for him.

"The troops' morale over here is very, very high," he said at the time. "They feel good about what they're doing over here. They know they have the support of the overwhelming majority of the American people.

"And, of course," he added, "feeling good about themselves helps them to do their job better. And it helps them to put up with all the suffering they've had to put up with."

To keep morale high,
Schwarzkopf often visited his troops.

"He's a legend over here," said one soldier. "All the guys in the field love him."

His troops were ready for battle. But Schwarzkopf admitted he would not be disappointed if the Iraqis voluntarily withdrew from Kuwait.

"I don't want to see one more American die," he said at the time. "There's no bloodlust on the part of myself or anybody else around here. What we want to do is accomplish the objectives of this whole thing, get it over as quickly as we can, and get back home."

President Bush set a January 15, 1991, deadline for Iraq to withdraw from Kuwait. The Iraqis ignored the deadline.

On January 16, President Bush gave Schwarzkopf the order to begin Operation Desert Storm. The general directed the war from his map-filled war room in Riyadh, Saudi Arabia. Operation Desert Storm began as an air war. No ground troops were sent in to expel the Iraqis from Kuwait. Nor were they sent to invade Iraq.

Schwarzkopf hoped to cripple Iraq's ability to wage war while sparing its citizens. He also hoped the Allied air force would soften the Iraqi defenses before the ground troops were sent in. This way, the Allies would suffer fewer casualties.

"We don't want to win the war and lose the peace," Schwarzkopf said at the time. "That's why we're in this coalition. That's why the rules of engagement we have are such." Schwarzkopf wasn't interested in wreaking mass destruction upon the entire nation of Iraq.

The air attacks lasted for weeks. Now it was time to drive the Iraqis from Kuwait.

On February 23, 1991, President Bush gave Schwarzkopf the go-ahead to begin the ground war. It lasted just 100 hours. Schwarzkopf's decision to out-flank the Iraqis with lightning-fast armored divisions proved to be the decisive move.

Schwarzkopf was proud of the way his men fought. But there wasn't a time he didn't worry about their lives.

"Every waking and sleeping moment," he told reporters, "my nightmare is the fact that I will give an order that will cause countless numbers of human beings to lose their lives. I don't want my troops to die. I don't want my troops to be maimed.

"It's an intensely personal, emotional thing for me," he added. "Any decision you have to make that involves the loss of human life is nothing you do lightly. I agonize over it."

A (Media) Star Is Born

During the air war, Schwarzkopf often appeared on television to tell the nation about the war's progress. But not until his final briefing on February 27—during the final hours of the war—did the 6-foot-3, 240-pound Schwarzkopf become America's hero. Not since World War II's General Dwight D. Eisenhower had there been such a visible or imposing military presence.

Dressed in his uniform, the burly 56-year-old Schwarzkopf dazzled the press and the nation with his wit, intelligence, and confidence. His comments were blunt, honest, and direct. He skillfully handled the difficult and sometimes stupid questions from reporters. He was the general. He was in charge. He knew what he was doing.

Schwarzkopf's news conference made him famous.

One reporter asked him what he thought of Saddam
Hussein as a military strategist. Schwarzkopf grinned
and replied: "He is neither a strategist nor is he
schooled in the operational arts. Nor is he a tactician.
Nor is he a general. Nor is he a soldier. Other than
that, he's a great military man."

Schwarzkopf also knew when to be serious. Desert Storm was a huge success. But Schwarzkopf had to remind himself—and the nation—that the deadly battle was still raging.

"I should remind you," he said to the press, "even as we speak, there is fighting going on. Even as we speak, there are incredible acts of bravery."

Desert Storm ended at midnight on February 27, 1991. On March 3, Schwarzkopf met with Iraqi commanders in a tent in U.S.-occupied southern Iraq. There the Iraqis agreed to exchange prisoners of war (POWs).

Schwarzkopf visited the American POWs once they were safely in U.S. hands. All the POWs were in good condition. But one soldier, 20-year-old Melissa A. Rathbun-Nealy, was strangely silent. The Iraqis had captured Nealy while she retrieved Allied vehicles in the Saudi Arabian desert. The Iraqis did not harm her. But she still went through tough times.

*Schwarzkopf greeted former prisoners of war
after they arrived from Iraq.*

Schwarzkopf tried to find the right words to comfort her.
But nothing worked. Finally, he said, "Melissa, would
you mind if I gave you a hug?"

Nealy's eyes brightened. "No," she replied, "I'd like that."

Said one observer, "She just grabbed on and hugged him.
And then everything was fine."

Schwarzkopf's efforts during the Persian Gulf War made him a hero and a household name. His personal pride returned. He restored the pride of an entire nation. The bad memories of the Vietnam War had finally disappeared.

"He's a natural on TV," said a television executive. "He exudes the perfect combination of confidence, authority, strength, warmth and humor. He's the father figure of the war."

"If Central Casting had tried to find the perfect general to star in a movie about resurrecting pride in America," said a television reporter, "it would have come up with Norman Schwarzkopf. He was John Wayne taking on the Iraqis."

Taking America By Storm

Schwarzkopf did not return to his home at MacDill Air
Force Base in Tampa, Florida, until April 21, 1991.
When he did, he discovered that his life had changed.

Before the Persian Gulf War, only military observers
knew Schwarzkopf's name.   Now he was "Stormin'
Norman"—American hero. At the air base, a large
crowd gathered to greet the general. Schwarzkopf,
still in battle fatigues, stepped off the airplane.
Suddenly, the crowd cheered wildly.

Then the Army band played the national anthem.
With tears in his eyes, Schwarzkopf stood at attention
and saluted. "It's a great day to be a soldier," he said.

After his triumphant return, Schwarzkopf met
the Queen of England at the White House.

But that was only the beginning. The President
invited Schwarzkopf to the White House for meetings
and photograph sessions. Then he attended a
black-tie dinner in his honor. Schwarzkopf met
England's Queen Elizabeth. He received over 700
interview requests.

Schwarzkopf was all smiles
at a black-tie dinner in Washington, D.C.

Publishers offered him multi-million dollar book deals. Some of America's top corporations offered him jobs. Schwarzkopf's picture appeared on the cover of many major magazines. Reporters wrote countless articles about him.

ABC-TV's Barbara Walters interviewed Schwarzkopf on a two-part "20/20" series. Letters and gifts poured in from all over America. Everywhere Schwarzkopf went, autograph seekers mobbed him.

Schwarzkopf took it all in stride. He felt honored that he had the chance to serve his country well. He turned down many offers. But there was one event Schwarzkopf wouldn't miss. He attended the parade honoring the troops of Operation Desert Storm.

Schwarzkopf proudly led a military parade down
Constitution Avenue in Washington, D.C.

The official Welcome Home celebration occurred June 15, 1991, in Washington, D.C. Schwarzkopf led more than 8,000 troops down Constitution Avenue to the Pentagon. Nearly 200,000 flag-wavers cheered as M1A1 tanks rumbled by and Stealth fighters flew overhead.

A week later, Schwarzkopf and his men were in New York City. There they received a ticker-tape parade. Schwarzkopf enjoyed it all. But he remained humble.

"I'm not a hero," he said. "It doesn't take a hero to order men into battle. It takes a hero to be one of those men. Those are the people who should receive adulation."

With his wife, Brenda, at his side, Schwarzkopf enjoys a ticker-tape parade in New York City.

At Ease, General

After 35 years of service, Norman Schwarzkopf retired from the Army in August 1991. He wanted to return to a normal family life. Schwarzkopf is close to his family and his black Labrador retriever, Bear. The 239 days he spent overseas was the longest he had been away from them in quite some time.

"I'm looking forward to a little time off," he said, "doing relaxing things with my family, getting my act together."

Schwarzkopf loves to fly-fish and shoot sporting clays. After he left the military, he took his son Christian on a hunting and fishing trip to Alaska.

Schwarzkopf doesn't wear his battle fatigues anymore. These days, he dresses in sport shirts and slacks. And he wears only one wristwatch now—not two like he did during the war. "I'm back on one time," he said with laughter. "I don't need to know what time it is in Riyadh anymore."

Schwarzkopf also likes to play tennis on weekends. He has a fondness for food. So he works out on exercise equipment in his garage. Some of his favorite foods include thick, rare steaks and mint-chocolate-chip ice cream.

"He knows he's fat," said an assistant. "Losing weight has been a New Year's resolution for a few years now."

At night, the Schwarzkopfs often gather to play games like "Trivial Pursuit" or "Win, Lose or Draw." "We don't like to play with him," said Brenda. "He always wins."

His favorite television shows are *Cheers* and
America's Funniest Home Videos. He also likes
Clint Eastwood Westerns and Charles Bronson mov-
ies, as well as opera and magic tricks.

Though Schwarzkopf has retired, his future looks
bright. Some people want him to run for political
office. But his family is against the idea. "The type of
politics I have in mind is being Mayor of a small
town," he said.

Schwarzkopf will write a book about his Persian Gulf
experiences and go on a lecture tour. Some say he
will receive as much as $4.5 million for his book and
$50,000 per speech. After that, Schwarzkopf will
involve himself with causes.

"The things I feel very strongly about are education,
the war on drugs, the environment and conservation
and wildlife," he said.

Will Schwarzkopf run for political office? Time will tell.

Will he miss the Army?

"People have the wrong idea about generals," he said. "They think we have our stars tattooed on us. But believe it or not, when I go to bed, I wear pajamas. I wear civilian clothes a lot, and I think I'll be very comfortable.

I'll find action," he added. "There's always plenty if you're willing to step into the fray."

H. Norman Schwarzkopf—hero of Operation Desert Storm.

GLOSSARY

ALLIED—United to fight a common enemy.

ARTILLERY—Large firing weapons such as cannons, howitzers, and missile launchers that are served by military crews.

BATTALION—A large military unit consisting of a headquarters company and four infantry companies and/or artillery batteries.

CASUALTIES—People injured, killed, captured, or missing in action against an enemy.

COUP—A sudden action taken by rebels to overthrow a country's leader or government.

FRIENDLY FIRE—When troops are killed by their own firepower, officially known as "fratricide."

MINEFIELD—An area in which explosive mines have been anchored or sunk in water or buried on land.

NAPALM—A soap of fatty acids that when mixed with gasoline makes a flammable jelly used in flamethrowers and bombs.

OPERATION DESERT SHIELD—The code word for the military action taken by U.S. and Allied troops to defend Saudi Arabia from possible invasion by Iraq.

OPERATION DESERT STORM—The code word for the military action taken by U.S. and Allied troops against the Iraqi Army in Kuwait and Iraq.